T0315828

CAN I START AGAIN PLEASE

Sue MacLaine

CAN I START AGAIN PLEASE

OBERON BOOKS
LONDON

WWW.OBERONBOOKS.COM

First published in 2016 by Oberon Books Ltd
521 Caledonian Road, London N7 9RH
Tel: +44 (0) 20 7607 3637 / Fax: +44 (0) 20 7607 3629
e-mail: info@oberonbooks.com
www.oberonbooks.com

A catalogue record for this book is available from the British
Library.

PB ISBN: 9781783193356

Cover photo by Matthew Andrews

Visit www.oberonbooks.com to read more about all our books
and to buy them. You will also find features, author interviews and
news of any author events, and you can sign up for e-newsletters
so that you're always first to hear about our new releases.

Author Notes

The play is for two performers[1] and is performed in British Sign Language[2] and spoken English.

The script is a character in the play and the performers are in a constantly active relationship with it.

This published text contains both the English and the BSL scripts which appear on the scroll used onstage[3].

The bracketed numbers indicate the number of seconds the performer pauses before continuing to speak.

The Wittgenstein quotes are spoken but not rendered in sign language. They are displayed in (hand)written form on large pieces of paper.

The capitalisation of certain words within the spoken English text indicates the performer is signing them.

By and large signed languages are not written and there is no standard way of writing them down. There is no formal written version of BSL. The script was first written in English and then a translation team of two native and two non-native sign language users worked for five days to create the core BSL script. This was recorded initially on film and then transposed into written form by Nadia Nadarajah.

Further information about transcription and notation systems for signed languages can be found at the Deafness, Cognition and Language Research Centre.

1 The performer delivering the script in sign language must be Deaf
2 It would be possible for the script to be translated into other signed languages as British Sign Language is not universal.
3 The two scripts are joined together to create a scroll and are continuously referred to and moved throughout the performance.

[HELLO].   [GOOD EVENING].   [WELCOME].   [THANK YOU].

        (point to the paper)   _____smile_(receptive)_____
[START] [QUOTE] WITTGENSTEIN [ME+PAUSE] [GOT+IT]

_____Qu_____   ____(nod) mmm____
[SHOULD] [TELL] [BRIEF]   [SOMETIMES][HELP] [ADD+++]

__smile_____(receptive)
 [ME+PAUSE] [GOT+IT]

_____(point)_____confirmed?_____
[HIM+EXPECT+KNOW+IT] [W++][DON'T KNOW].

_____(fs)_____   _umm?___
W.I.T.T.G.E.N.S.T.E.I.N.   [REALLY]

           _(point to brain)___
[QUESTION][DIRECT] [DON'T PROCESS]

[ASK+YOU]

[DISCUSS+YOU++]   [QUESTION+ASK+YOU]

           _____Qu___
[ASK+YOU] [W++] [KNOWLEDGE], [CONCEPT+ANYTHING],

[KNOW+++]

____(point at script)_____(break)
[HERE] [THINK++] [SPEAK+OUT] [LACK].

_____(break)
[HERE] [THINK] [PROCESS] [LACK]

____(become child)_____(past)_____(age)
[THIS+CHILD] [HAPPEN+ME] [BEFORE] [ME] [6]

[LATER] [ME+TELL+YOU].

Hello. Good evening. Welcome and thank you.

I will start with a quote from Wittgenstein and I will just pause
while that is translated. (3)

Wittgenstein   W.i.t.t.g.e.n.s.t.e.i.n
Should I say a little about him?
Would that help? Sometimes it does.
Context.
I'll just pause while that is interpreted (6)

It cannot be presumed that we all know who Wittgenstein,
w.i.t.t.g.e.n.s.t.e.i.n, is.
Can it? (2)

It is a direct question
Don't translate that.

I am asking you

I am talking to you all.
I am asking you a question (1)

I am asking whether knowledge of Wittgenstein, or indeed
anything, can be presumed.

We are thinking here about when language fails. We are
thinking about what cannot be said, especially by a child,
especially by a child, and I was 6 years old but I will come to
that later.

(point) _____fs_____
[W++] W.I.T.T.G.E.N.S.T.E.I.N

__mm_Qu ___(point)____Qu___ ____(nod)_confirmed_
[SHOULD] [BRIEF] [TELL+YOU] [OR][EXPECT][KNOW++].

[W++].

(point)_____Qu___ _____ah___
[NAME][NEED][SPELL][AGAIN] [NO] [SEEM] [YOU+KNOW].

_Qu__
[HOW++THAT] [WELL]

[SPELL] [SAME+THIS] [W++]

[PROCESS?]

[ASK+YOU]

[QUESTION+ASK+YOU]

[ME+QUESTION+ASK][YOU+PROCESS+THIS].

_no_(smile)
[NEED]

[ASK+YOU] [SPELL] [W++] [HOW].

[SHOW+ME]

[SHOW+EVERYONE] [COME+ON]

[ONCE] [YOU+SPELL] [WHAT+THAT+MEAN]

(point)[VOO(don't know)].

[W++] [VOO(don't know)].

[WHAT+YOU+IMAGINE]?

[PERSON] [YOU+DON'T+KNOW]

[PERSON] [UMM(really)] [YOU+DON'T+KNOW]

[YOU+RECOGNISE] [ME+TELL] [IT'S+PERSON]

[HUMAN]

[WANT] [MAKE+SURE] [THIS+UNDERSTOOD]

Wittgenstein   W.i.t.t.g.e.n.s.t.e.i.n (3)

So should I?   Say a little about him?
Or presume we all know. About Wittgenstein. (1)

Do I need to spell it again? (1)   No it seems you have it. (3)

How do you do that? (1)   Is it?

Spell out a name like that.   Like Wittgenstein? (1)

Are you interpreting this? (3) I am asking you I am asking you the question

Are you interpreting my asking you the question. There's no need

I am asking you how you spell out a name such as Wittgenstein.

Could you show me? (1)   Show all of us? (3)

And once you've spelt it (1) What does it mean? (3)

If you don't know him. If you don't know Wittgenstein.

What can it possibly mean?
If you don't know the person
If you don't know it is a person (5)

Do they know I am talking about a person (1)
A human being? (1)

I want to make sure that is being communicated

[OPTIONS] [FACT] [YOU+DON'T+KNOW], [MOVE+ON] [HOW]?

__(placement)_____ __(can't)__ (look at audience)_____
[SIGN+++] [TRAUMA+++] [RELAY+++] (but) [ALL PROCESS++]

{A} [THAT+WHY] [SUGGEST] [ME+BRIEF+TELL+YOU].
[BETTER [GET+KNOW]

[W++] [IDEA] [CONCEPT] [LANDSCAPE].

__(point to the hand & stay) (signs then to the hand)__ (point to the hand)_
[PROPOSTION] [THIS] [KNOWLEDGE] [BELIEVE] [REMEMBER]
[THIS] [ACCEPT] [TRUE].

_(point)_____(under hand)____vee_____(confused)__
[W++] [TELL+YOU] [PROPOSTION] [LIST] [ADD+IN++] [NOTHING]
[MEANS] [WHAT]

_____(receptive)_
[ME+PAUSE] [GOT+IT]

[PUT+UP+WITH+IT] [TRUST] [ME+SIGN++] [POINT]
[TRANSLATE+TELL+YOU]

[SAME] [ME+STAND] [CLIFF+DOWN+GROUND+UP+CLIFF]

_(point to ground)_____(placement)_____
[THIS][NOT+SURE++] [ME+RUN+LEAP+HIGH] (cover my eyes
then peep out to the audience)

[HAVE] [QUIZ] [AFTERWARDS]

[QUIZ] [WHAT'S FOR] [MAKE+SURE] [THIS+UNDERSTAND]

[MAKE+SURE] [YOU+UNDERSTAND] [MY+MEANS]

[DON'T+PROCESS]

(shake head) [NEED]

[THIS+JOKE]

[THIS+QUIZ]

How can anything be understood if the very basic facts are not known? (5)

There are words and there is trauma and the words cannot explain the trauma but we are here trying to find a translation (5)

That's why I thought to say a little about him. Rather than presuming

About Wittgenstein and this idea of context.   Of landscape.

A proposition is something known or believed or remembered that is proposed for acceptance as true.

Wittgenstein said a proposition has no meaning unless it is placed in its proper context

I'll just give time for that to be interpreted (5)

SUE and NADIA look at each other.

I am going to have to trust that you are rendering my meaning accurately

Take a leap of faith.   We all are.

A leap of faith across a gulf of doubt (6)

There will be a quiz afterwards.

A quiz to ensure comprehension has occurred

To ensure you have understood my meaning (2)

Don't translate that (1)

There's no need (1)

It was a joke (1)

About the quiz (8)

[W++] [SAID]

[THIS + OPTIONS]…….. [TRANSLATION MEANS].

[YOU+DON'T+KNOW] [SIGNS+FROZEN] [SH+]

[OR]

[NOTHING] [SIGN(say)] (stammered)   [SILENT (peace)+]

[PREFER] [WHICH?]

[MAYBE] (point to audience) [YOU] [HAVE] [OWN] [VIEWS]
(signs reached audience)

[TELL+ME?] (shake head) [HOLD+ON (don't care)]
(signs reached audience)

[SH+]   [SILENT (peace)+]   [SHUT+IT]

[WANT] [SAY]. [HERE] [IMPORTANT].   [YOU PROCESS++].

[HERE] [EVENING] [HAPPEN] [BAD] [NOTHING].
[EVERYTHING] [ALREADY]

[HAPPENED (past)].   [HERE] [AIM] [HAPPEN+AFTER]
[WAVES (carry+on)++].

[PLANE+CRASH] [TEDDY+BEAR (describe)] [EARS++ WAVES]
[WRECKAGE++].

[HERE] [AIM] [HAPPEN+AFTER]; [GRASS (describe)+
MOVE (fingertips)+++]

[CROP+OFF (fingertips bend down++)].

[HERE+EVENING] [HAPPEN] [BAD] [NOTHING].
[ALL+CONFIRM (fine)].

[YOU+SAFE].   [ME+LOVE+YOU]. [HAPPEN+HERE]
[BOTH-OF-US] [SECRET].

Wittgenstein said

'WHEREOF ONE CANNOT SPEAK THEREOF ONE MUST BE SILENT'

In other words … and this may help.   In the translation. (1)
'If you don't know how to say it, then be quiet' (8)
Or

'If you have nothing to say then keep silent' (8)
Which do you prefer? (1)
Or maybe you have your own thoughts on the meaning (1)

In which case keep them to yourself

Be quiet   Keep silent   Shut it

Choreographic sequence.

I also want to say.
And this you can translate.
This is important.

Nothing bad will happen here.
Everything bad has already happened.
This is the aftermath.

The flip-flop washed up on the shore.
The teddy bear, the teddy bear in the wreckage.

This is the aftermath; the second crop of grown grass after the first
has been harvested.

Nothing bad will happen to you this evening.
Nothing at all.
You are safe here. I love you.
What happens here will be our little secret.
(Stand and sit.) I LOVE YOU   *(Stand and sit.)*

(Placement of quiet and silence)

[SH+] [PEACE] [OF+COURSE] DIFFERENT.

[DIFFERENT] [HOW?]

__fs____   _____fs____
[Q.U.I-E.T]   [S.I.L.E.N.C.E]

[INTERPRET] [HOW?] [SHOW+ME] [SHOW+EVERYONE]
[COME+ON]

_____fs_____
[S.I.L.E.N.C.E]

___fs____
[Q.U.I.E.T]

[AH] [YOU] [SIGN THIS+++(placement)] [WHY?]

[PROCESS+DON'T!].

[ASK] [SIGN THIS++] [PROCESS+DON'T!]

[THIS+CONVERSATION] [PRIVATE].

[BOTH-OF-US+++]

[THESE+OPTIONS (list)++]

[EACH++] [DIFFERENT] (signs reach toward audience)

[DEPEND] [OWN (sign toward audience)] [LIFE+EXPERIENCE]

(signs on head level) [OPEN+DRAWER++]
[INFO+COME+ME+IN+++]

           __vee__   _____poo_____
[INFO+IN] [DIDN'T] [YOU+DON'T-UNDERSTAND
(over the head)]

[DRAWER+CLOSE++] [WORM+CONNECT++ (like machine)].

(Placement) [WORLD] [ME (index)] [LINK (connect)].

[LINK] + (move left to right and repeat) + (here to future)
+ (here to past)

[ME+GROW-UP]+[LOOK-AROUND++]
[ME+GROW-UP]+[LEARN++]

And we have to acknowledge that 'quiet' and 'silence'
are of course completely different words.

How different are they?

Quiet and Silence

How do you interpret the difference?
Can you show me? (1)   Show all of us? (3)

Silence

Quiet
Choreographic sequence.

Could you say a little about the contextualising influences
on your choices

Don't translate that. (2)

Don't translate my asking about the contextualising influences (2)

That's a private conversation. (2)

Between you and me (4)

There are so many possibilities (1)

For each person it will be quite different

Dependent on their life experience

Your schematic expectations influence which data is encoded
and retained

The brain will make infinitesimal adjustments, minute calibrations
Assimilating and accommodating.

Allowing continuous adaptations to the self and the world.

Back and forth   Back and forth   Here and there Now and then
Orientating the world

Giving a sense of predictability
A sense of continuity

[ME+GROW-UP]+[EXPECT++]

[YOUR+EXPERIENCE] [SAME (point at placement)?]

[YOU+CHILDHOOD+TELL+ME] [NO+NEED].
[SAME] [ME+TELL+YOU] (shake head)

[NOW] [THINK++ (rub chin)] [WHAT+YOU+WORK-OUT]

(handshapes of '5' close)

[LOOK+ME] [DISCUSS++]

[INTERPRET+DON'T]

[CHIN+UP] [FOCUS] [BLUNT] [CHIN+UP] [LOOK+ME]

[LOOK+ME]. [ME+WORLD]

[GO-AWAY+++]

[GO-AWAY+] .   [THIS+NOW].   [YOU+ME++++]

[STOP+INTERPRET] [PLEASE] [DISCUSS++]

[STOP+INTERPRET] [PLEASE].

(handshapes of 'link') [RELATIONSHIP?]   [ME+W+YOU?]
[W+ME+YOU].

('timeline' from past to now) [HARD??] (nod)
[APOLOGIES]
('timeline' from now to future) [HARD] ('confirmation' nod)

[SHOPPING] [FOOD (item)] ['action' SELF-CHECK]
(item isn't working) [ABSTRACT] [THROW+AWAY]
[(point) WHAT'S IT?]

(point) [ABSTRACT] (point) [NAUGHTY]

[ABSTRACT] [EASY] [UNDERSTAND] ('confirmation' nod).

Was that your experience growing up? (1)

I don't need your life history.   And you don't need mine

I just need to know what you are making of all this (1)
What are you making of all this?

Looking at me would be helpful. While we talk.

Don't translate that (2)

Chin up   I'm talking to you   Directly to you   Chin up

Look at me Look directly at me.

I am your world. It doesn't matter if everyone understands.

It doesn't matter.

This now.

This now is just between you and me

Can you please pause the translation while I talk to you (1)

Can you please stop translating.

Are you still with me?
With me and Wittgenstein?
Wittgenstein and I.
This must be all quite hard now. (1)

My apologies.   It is going to get worse (3)

Unexpected item in the bagging area
That came out of nowhere
No clue
No hint

Completely unexpected
That was naughty
(Repeat NAUGHTY.) x8

The sentence 'unexpected item in the bagging area' is easy
enough to understand.
You know what the sentence means but the problem will lie in
your grasping my intention.

[YOU+KNOW] [ABSTRACT] [MEANS] ('confirmation' nod)
[YOU+KNOW] [WHY??]

[ABSTRACT] ('confirmation' shake the head).

[ABSTRACT++++] (from small to big space).

[STOP]

[STOP]

[PAUSE] (nod)

(Placement of pause and stop) [PAUSE]   [STOP] [DIFFERENT] (nod)

[INTERPRET] [HOW?]

[SHOW+ME]   [SHOW+EVERYONE] [COME+ON]

[ME MOVE+ON+++] [ABSTRACT] (ignore) [MOVE+ON+++]
[ABSTRACT] (ignore)

(point to head) [COME+IN++++] (from slow to faster)
(grab hand of point to the head and look at it)

[STOP+IT]

[HOLD+BREATH]   [BREATH++]

[DIRECT+YOU].

[TELL+YOU]

[PROCESS] [NO+NEED]

[DIRECT+YOU+TELL+YOU]

[WONDER] [YOU+NO] [LISTEN+ME] [WHY??]

[WANT+YOU] [LISTEN+ME] [HOW?]

[HOLD+BREATH]   [BREATH] [ALL+HOLD+BREATH]
[ALL+BREATH]

[WORDS+++] (location – mouth) [SIGNS++++]

[INFO+GRAB+PULL+IN(brain)++++]

[GRAB+INFO+PULL+AWAY++++] (signs in slow motion).

There is competing information.

There is the sentence, there is the meaning of the sentence and there is the intention of the sentence.

Choreographic sequence.

I suggest you pause

Not stop

I didn't say stop I said pause PAUSE   [N] PAUSE

They are quite different Pause and Stop (1)

How do you interpret the difference? (3)

Can you show me (1)   Show all of us (3)

Unexpected information can throw the whole system off balance
The mind is caught in a quandary

There is the compulsion to complete the process of knowing and the fear of doing so

What to do (1)

Hold your breath if necessary (3)   Or keep breathing (3)

That's directly to you   I am saying it to you

You don't need to translate that (3)   I'm saying it directly to you

And I can only wonder why you are not listening to me.

What do I have to say to make you listen to me?

Hold your breath   Catch your breath
Catch my breath   Catch all our breaths
These words spill out, roll out, tumble out and you are holding on. (1)
Barely. (1)

[W++SAID]

(Repeat signs in face expression from happy to sad)
[LOOK+AT] [LAMP(describe)]

[LOOK+AT] [LAMP(describe)] [LOOK+AT] [LAMP(describe)]
[LOOK+AT] [LAMP(describe)].

[LIGHT+OFF].   [FADE+AWAY].

[LAMP+FADE+AWAY] [BED+FADE+AWAY] [PILLOW+FADE+AWAY]
[SHEET+FADE+AWAY] [ROOM+FADE+AWAY]
[HOUSE+FADE+AWAY]
[STREET+FADE+AWAY] [TOWN+FADE+AWAY] [SEA+FADE+AWAY]
[SKY+FADE+AWAY] [STARS+FADE+AWAY] [SISTER+WALK+AWAY]
[MOTHER+WALK+AWAY] [FATHER+WALK+AWAY]
[WORLD+FADE+AWAY]

You are barely holding on (2)
The working memory is in overdrive; shedding information as
quickly as possible, holding onto the echo memory of the last
few words, the last few sounds. (12)

Wittgenstein said

> 'ONE CANNOT SPEAK THE TRUTH IF ONE HAS NOT
> YET CONQUERED ONESELF. THE TRUTH CAN BE SPOKEN
> ONLY BY SOMEONE WHO IS ALREADY AT HOME IN IT,
> NOT BY SOMEONE WHO STILL LIVES IN UNTRUTHFULNESS
> AND DOES NO MORE THAN REACH OUT TOWARDS IT
> FROM WITHIN UNTRUTHFULNESS'.

I looked at the lamp on the bedside table and I said lamp
And I said it again
And I said it again and I continued until finally the lamp was
un-lamped.
De-lamped.
No longer a lamp.

There was no longer a lamp.
There was no longer a bed, no longer a pillow, no longer a sheet,
no longer a room, no longer a house, no longer a street, no longer
a town, no longer the sea, no longer the sky, no longer the stars,
no longer a sister, no longer a mother, no longer a father, no
longer the world. (4)

[ROMAN] [THEIR] [TRANSLATION] [MEANS]
[HE (point)+ DISCLOSE+THINK] [AGREE] ('confirmation' nod)

_____fs_____
[ME+LIKE] [TELL+YOU] [CLARIFY(language)] [MEANS] M.E.S.S.A.G.E
[AIMS] [MEANS] [OR] [W+TELL+YOU]

(point at the sheet) [GIGGLES ('confirmation' nod++)]

[YOU+THINK] [FUNNY(point)] [UNDERSTAND?++]

[CHEEKY]

[CAN+YOU] [THIS+GIVE+MESSAGE] [PLEASE].
[HUMOUR] [ME+WAIT]

[THINK+ABOUT+++] (placement) [FUNNY+LEVEL]
[FUNNY+LEVEL] [EQUAL?].

[TAKE+TIME]

'QUI TACIT CONSENTIT VIDETEUR' (5)
There is a Roman proverb which translated means;
he who keeps silent is assumed to consent (4)

Bell Ring

I would like to speak now about language meaning and
message meaning or as Wittgenstein would say
LET THE USE OF WORDS TEACH YOU THEIR
MEANING (7)
or
TELL ME HOW YOU ARE SEARCHING AND I WILL
TELL YOU WHAT YOU ARE SEARCHING FOR(7)
or
WHEN WE CAN NO LONGER THINK FOR
OURSELVES WE CAN ALWAYS QUOTE

Do you think it is understood that the last point was humorous

Tongue in cheek
Does that translate? (6)

Could you convey it now please   The humour   I'll wait

Take your time in thinking about how best to achieve
the equivalence.

Take your time (5)

[HAVE] [STORY]. [WELL+KNOWN] [(umm) TRUE+OR+FALSE]
[DON'T+KNOW].

[YOU+KNOW] [AMERICAN] [PRESIDENT] R.E.A.G.A.N
[FIRST+TIME] [FLY] [WHERE+RUSSIA] [WHAT'S+FOR?] [AIMS]
[NUCLEAR+BOMBS] [WIPE+OUT].

[CONFERENCE+DISCUSS+AGREE+SIGNED] [PRESIDENT]
[GIVE+SPEECH] [SAY+THANKS] [ALMOST+END]
[TELL+JOKE] [WHAT?] [FARMERS + COWBOYS].

[INTERPRETER+RUSSIA] [KNEW] [JOKES+THEIR+AMERICAN]
[IGNORE+TWIST] [TELL+WHAT?] [JOKES+THEIR+RUSSIAN]
[WHAT?] [VODKA + ALL+DAY+WINTER].

[ALL+LAUGH(handshapes '5' bends)] [PRESIDENT] [SMILE]
[THAT'S+IT+WANT]

[RUSSIAN+IMPRESSED] [EVERYTHING+OK].

[GO+ON+++OK?]   [WANT+ME] [REPEAT?++]

[ME+SIGN+FAST+ME+TELL+ME?]
[(point)+TOLD+ME+SIGN+TOO+FAST]

[GO+ON+++OK?]   [WANT+ME] [REPEAT?++]

[ME+SIGN+FAST+ME+TELL+ME?]
[(point)+TOLD+ME+SIGN+TOO+FAST]

[SIGNS+++ CAN'T+HELP+IT]

[STORY] [TELL+YOU] (placement) [CLARIFY(language)]
[MEANS] [AIMS(message)] [MEANS].

[JOKES] (placement) [AMERICAN] [RUSSIAN] [THEIR].

[AIMS(message)] [AMERICAN+PRESIDENT] [WANT+YOU]
[LIKE+ME](tap shoulder++).

[WORDS+OUT++(location- mouth)] [OPEN+LIST+ADD++]

[THAT'S+IT] [WANT] [GIVE+MESSAGE]. [THAT'S+IT] [WANT]
[UNDERSTOOD].

There is a story, I am uncertain if it is apocryphal.

President Reagan was visiting Russia for the first time after signing a treaty that eliminated a whole class of nuclear weapons from Europe.

At the end of a summit meeting, Reagan gave a speech of thanks ending with a joke about farmers and cowboys.

The Russian interpreter knew the joke to be untranslatable and so decided to tell a Russian joke instead. He ignored completely what Reagan said and went ahead with his own joke about Vodka and long winter nights.

The joke was well received. Reagan got the big laugh he wanted and the Russian politicians were appreciative of his sense of humour.

All was well.

How are you getting on? Do you need me to repeat anything?

Tell me if I am speaking too fast?   I am told I speak too fast
How are you getting on? Do you need me to repeat anything?

Tell me if I'm speaking too fast   I am told I speak too fast

But am unable to change my behaviour (3)

The story demonstrates the difference between language meaning and message meaning. (1)
The language was the joke. (1)

The message was that Reagan wanted to be liked. (2)

Meaning is found from within the intention of the message.

That's what I want conveyed. That's what I want understood. (6)

[MUST+THINK++] [PERSON+SAY] [FOG/MIST] [GOT+IT].

[THEM+THINK+++]

(choreograph on placement)

I.F [WORD] (point) [JEWS(poo)]

I.F [LIST] [POSSIBLE+++]

[JOIN (but stuck)]   [WORD+GRAB+IN]   [JOIN+TOGETHER]

[DISCUSS (but stuck)]   [WORD+GRAB+IN]
[DISCUSS+AROUND(smoothly)]

[IMAGINE (but stuck)] [WORD+GRAB+IN]
[IMAGINE+OPEN(smoothly)]

[NARROW+MIND (but stuck)] [WORD+GRAB+IN]
[OPEN+MIND(smoothly)]

[LOOK+INSIDE (shake head)] [WORD+GRAB+IN]
[PULL+LOOK+INSIDE (nod)]

[INSIDE+YOU+LOOK+AT (stuck)] [WORD+GRAB+IN]
[LOOK+AT (nod) YOU+KNOW]

[DOOR] [KNOB+STUCK] [WORD+GRAB+IN][OPEN+DOOR]

[LOOK+AT (nod)]

[YOU+CAN] [TRANSLATE+THIS] [PLEASE].
[ONCE] [LONG+TIME+AGO]. [ME+REMEMBER]
[ME+WAKE+UP] [WANT+TOILET]. [ME+REMEMBER]
[ME+DOWNSTAIRS] [DON'T+WANT].

[YOU+CAN] [TRANSLATE+THIS] [PLEASE].
[ONCE] [LONG+TIME+AGO]. [ME+REMEMBER]
[ME+WAKE+UP] [WANT+TOILET]. [ME+REMEMBER]
[ME+DOWNSTAIRS] [DON'T+WANT].

You have to know what someone is trying to say.
What they are thinking

We rely here on the word 'if'

On the possibility contained within the word 'if'
On the kindness of 'if'
The generosity of 'if'
The imagination of 'if'

If I imagine
If only for a moment
If you can imagine
If only for a moment

If I imagine what I remember is true

If you imagine what I remember is true

Imagine a locked door
'If' has the capacity to open it

Can you translate the following please.
Once upon a time a very long time ago.
I remember waking up and wanting to go to the toilet.
I remember not wanting to go downstairs.

Can you translate the following please
Once upon a time a very long time ago
I remember waking up and wanting to go to the toilet.
I remember not wanting to go downstairs.

[YOU+CAN] [TRANSLATE+THIS] [PLEASE]
[ME+REMEMBER] [ME+DOWNSTAIRS+BEEN]
[PROPOSITIONS] [THIS+ACCEPT] [TRUE] [WHAT?]
(Description) [HOUSE HAVE]. [STAIRS THERE].

[TOILET THERE]. [TOILET DOWNSTAIRS]

[HAPPENED] [LONG+TIME+AGO].
[YOU+IMAGINE] [WHAT?]
(Description) [HOUSE] [TWO+FLOORS]   [NIGHT+TIME].

[CHILD THERE]
[IMAGINE? (anything else)]
[IMAGINE? (anything else)]
[YOURS+PERSPECTIVES+++] [ACCEPT].

[ME+DESCRIBE] [WHAT'S+IT?]

[THINGS] [PILE] [MUST+SEPARATE] [IF+TOGETHER] [RISK]
[SEPARATE+GROUP++]

[THINGS+IN] (placement of 2 areas) [PRESS+BUTTONS+++]
[LOOK+AT (2 places)+++]

[THINGS+OUT++] [PILES+++]   [GRAB+TOGETHER]
[PUT+IT+IN] [PRESS+BUTTONS++++] [IT+OUT++]
[PILES+++] [REPEAT++++]

[KNOW+WHAT'S+IT] [LAUNDRY] L.A.U.N.D.R.Y [YES]
[THAT'S+IT+DESCRIPTION].

(nod) [SENSE (point to head)]. [HAVE WORD THERE (point to head)].

[PERSON+SIGN++] [WHAT'S+IT?] [AH+GOT+IT]

[WORD] L.A.U.N.D.R.Y [PULL+OUT] [THAT'S+IT]
[BECOME+CLEAR].
[WORDS+ALREADY+THERE (point to the head)]
[WAIT+++UNDERSTAND]

Can you translate the following please (10)
I remember going downstairs
What propositions did you accept as true?
There was a house
There were stairs

There was a toilet.
The toilet was downstairs
It happened a long time ago
What did you infer or imagine?

The house was on two floors
It was night time
It involved a child
Anything else?
Anything else?
All perspectives gratefully received. (1)

What is being described here?

First items are sorted in different groups or one group may
be sufficient

If you have the necessary facilities you can start or you may need
to go elsewhere
It is better to do a few things at at time rather than too many
as mistakes can easily happen.
After the procedure is completed the materials are arranged back
into their appropriate places and will eventually be used again
and so the whole cycle will be repeated.
It is unlikely that the need for this task will ever end. Laundry.
It was a description of doing the laundry.

Now it makes sense.
Now everything falls into place.
Because you already know it.
On some level you already know
The knowledge was stored but access denied until the word 'laundry'
And then all became clear.

It was there all the time; waiting to be understood.

[W+] I.F [WORD+GRAB+IN] [WRONG?]

(shake head) [PROCESS+DON'T].

[EMOTION(trauma)] [HORROR(extreme)] [MEANS+WHAT]
[PERSON] [POSSIBLE]
[RISK] [DEATH] [INJURY] [SERIOUS], [PERSON]
[COULD+ABSTRACT] [BECOME]
[FEAR] [NOT+SURE] [TUMMY+RUMBLE].

R.E.P.R.E.S.S.I.O.N [INFO+PUT+IN(brain)+LOCK]
D.I.S.S.O.C.I.A.T.I.O.N [INFO+IN++++] [THROW+AWAY]
(placement of repression and dissociation) [REPRESSION]
[DISSOCIATION] [OF+COURSE] [DIFFERENT]

[INTERPRET] [HOW?]

[SHOW+ME]   [SHOW+EVERYONE] [COME+ON]

(Repeat signs in face expression from happy to sad)

[LOOK+AT] [LAMP(describe)] [LOOK+AT] [LAMP(describe)]

[LOOK+AT] [LAMP(describe)] [LOOK+AT] [LAMP(describe)].

[LIGHT+OFF]. [FADE+AWAY].

[LAMP+FADE+AWAY] [BED+FADE+AWAY]
[PILLOW+FADE+AWAY]
[SHEET+FADE+AWAY] [ROOM+FADE+AWAY]
[HOUSE+FADE+AWAY] [STREET+FADE+AWAY]
[TOWN+FADE+AWAY] [SEA+FADE+AWAY] [SKY+FADE+AWAY]
[STARS+FADE+AWAY] [SISTER+WALK+AWAY]
[MOTHER+WALK+AWAY] [FATHER+WALK+AWAY]
[WORLD+FADE+AWAY]

Wittgenstein said

'WHAT CAN BE SAID AT ALL CAN BE SAID CLEARLY;
AND WHEREOF ONE CANNOT SPEAK
THEREOF ONE MUST BE SILENT' (1)

But what if Wittgenstein is wrong? (1)

Don't translate that.

Extreme trauma is that which involves threatened death or
serious injury or a threat to the physical integrity of the self
which results in intense fear, helplessness or horror.

Choreographic sequence.

Repression and dissociation are of course very different words

How do you interpret the difference?

Can you show me (1)   Show all of us (3)

[N&S]r.e.p.r.e.s.s.i.o.n   [S] Repression   [N&S] REPRESSION
[N&S] d.i.s.s.o.c.i.a.t.i.o.n [S] Dissociation [N&S] DISSOCIATION

I looked at the lamp on the bedside table and I said lamp
And I said it again
And I said it again and I continued until finally the lamp was
un-lamped.
De-lamped.
No longer a lamp.

There was no longer a lamp and there was no longer a bed,
no longer a pillow, no longer a sheet, no longer a room,
no longer a house, no longer a street, no longer a town,
no longer the sea, no longer the sky, no longer the stars,
no longer a sister, no longer a mother, no longer a father,
no longer the world.

[BRAIN (handshape and move to location–space)]
[LOOK+AT] [EVERYONE+LOOK+AT]

[BRAIN (like playing recorder)]

[BRAIN+OPEN] [LOOK+AT+EVERYONE+LOOK+AT]

[THAT'S+IT] [AGREE+ALL] (confirmation)

[(point) GIVE+MESSAGE+OUT]

[GIVE+MESSAGE] [MEANS] [TRUST+SHARE+++]

[MEANS] [GIVE+MESSAGE+UMMM(really)?] (point at the brain)

[WE+ALL] [SING++] [FROM] [SAME] [SONG] [SHEET]
(point at the brain?)

I.D.I.O.M [" "] [WHAT'S+IT?] [OR] [ME+SHOULD] [TELL+YOU]
[BRIEF?]

[LANGUAGE] [SIGNS++] [FROZEN(stuck)] [HIT+WALL?]
[SING+FROM+SAME+SONG+SHEET] [THAT] [" "].
(placement) [HAVE] [DIRECT] [TRANSLATION] [OR]
[NEED+EXPLAIN++]

[PROCESS] [PACE+++]   [NO+RUSH]   [PACE+++]

[PLENTY] [THINK+ABOUT++]. [PACE++++]

[SING+FROM+SAME+SONG+SHEET] [MEANS]
[ALL+AGREE++][TELL+YOU] [SAME] [SUBJECT].

[PUBLIC] [ALL-OF-US] [TELL+YOU] [ANSWER+SAME]
[EXPLAIN+SAME]

[ASK+ME++++]

[OF+COURSE] [ME+SECRET+KEEP(keep still)]
[HAVE+RIGHT(different placement)]

[WANT+YOU+LOOK+AT+ME] [ME+PROCESS] [TELL+YOU]

(placement) [THURSDAY] [FRIDAY]
[WILL+RAIN+ UMM(confirmed)] [EITHER]

[THURSDAY] [VEE(nothing)]

[MEANS] [FRIDAY] [UMM(really)] (confirmation)

[UMM(really)??]

We are constantly engaged in the act of sense-making
De-coding
Re-coding
We are constantly engaged in the act of sense-making
Co-constructing meaning
We are co-constructing meaning here tonight (1)
There is trust that the meaning is being conveyed.
Is the meaning being conveyed?
Are we all singing from the same song sheet.

'SINGING FROM THE SAME SONG SHEET' (2)
Do I need to say what an idiom is? Or can we take it as read? (1)
Have we reached the limits of language?
'Singing from the same song sheet' is an idiom.
Is there a direct translation for 'idiom' or are you needing to
explain what it is (1)
Take your time with the interpretation
Take your time. There's no rush.
There's been a lot to think about. We can all take a moment (3)

'Singing from the same song sheet' means everyone is in
agreement as to what is going to be said about a subject.
In public. We all give the same answer, the same explanation.

If anyone asks we all say 'she fell over'

It is of course our right to remain silent. To say nothing at all.

What inference can be drawn by the following
Either it rained on Thursday or on Friday.

There was no rain on Thursday.
Therefore it rained on Friday
Would you agree that is a correct inference?(4)

(placement) [THURSDAY] [FRIDAY]
[WILL+RAIN+ UMM(confirmed)] [EITHER]
[THURSDAY] [VEE(nothing)]
[MEANS] [FRIDAY] [UMM(really)] (confirmation)
[UMM(really)??] (look at handshape)

[KEEP+SECRET] (move forward then move backward) [SECRET+OUT]
[AGREE] (move forward then move backward) [DISAGREE]
[TELL+STORY+++] [STORY+BACKWARD] [SPEAK+OUT]
[SECRET] (hold long) [SECRET+OUT]
[REMEMBER] (hold long) [FORGET]
[TRY+TO+FORGET+++] (stop) [REMEMBER]

[OVERALL+IN(point at the hand)] [RULES] [WELL??] FOR+YOU]

[DISCUSS+YOU++]. [DIRECT+YOU].

[ME+SECRET] (shake head) [MUST+INFORM](keep still)
(point at handshape) [VEE(didn't)] [YOU+ALL]
[SUSPICIOUS (at handshape)]
[SECRET] I.F [WORD+GRAB+IN] [(stand up) SPEAK+OUT]
[DISCUSS+YOU++]. [ME+ASK+YOU+BELIEVE+ME?]

What inference can be drawn by the following
Either it rained on Thursday or on Friday.
There was no rain on Thursday.
Therefore it rained on Friday
Would you agree that is a correct inference?(4)

If later I say something I didn't say before …
If later I stop singing from the same song sheet …
If later I tell a different story
If later I break the silence
If my speech rises out of silence, my remembering from forgetting

What would be the correct inference ?
For you
I'm talking to you now.
Directly to you.

We no longer have the right to remain silent.
We have to speak because if we don't, then later, it will be asked;
Why didn't we speak at the very first opportunity
So what does my silence say? To you?
I am talking to you now. I am asking if you believe me?

SUE MACLAINE

NADIA speaks and SUE signs.

Sometimes I forget you are there

You are an invisible presence

But then, out of the corner of my eye, I see you and I think, oh there she is again

Waiting to be rescued.

Boo hoo.

Stupid bitch

Stupid cow

Who the fuck do you think you are

Get up

I said get up

I'm talking to you now

Get here

Get over here

I'm talking to you

Directly to you

This is nobody else's business

It's just between you and me.

[BEFORE] [CHRISTMAS] (placement) [ME+STAND+TOP]
[STAIRS] [DAD] [DOWNSTAIRS] (role-shift) [WAVE+AT+DAD]
[ME+COME+DOWN] (role-shift) [NOT+YET] (role-shift & giggles)
[ME+STEP+DOWN] [WAVE+AT+DAD] [ME+COME+DOWN]
(role-shift) [NOT+YET] (role-shift & giggles) [ME+STEP+DOWN]
[WAVE+AT+DAD] [ME+COME+DOWN] (role-shift)
[NOT+YET] (role-shift & giggles) [ME+STEP+DOWN]
[FINALLY] [ME+ON+GROUND] [LOOK+UP] [JAW+DROP]
[SEE+TABLE] [PRESENTS++++++ PILES] [HALF+FOR+ME]
[HALF+FOR+MY+SISTER]. [BEFORE] [FAMILY] [NICE]

[GO+ON][OK?]
[PREPARE] [OK?]
(placement) [IMAGINE] [IMAGINE] [MATCH?]

(placement) [CRAWL+OUT+HEAD+OUT]
[YOU+CRAWL+OUT+HEAD+OUT] [SAME?]
(placement) [THINK+LIST] [YOU+LIST] [FIT+TOGETHER?]

[DISCUSS+YOU++]. [DIRECT+YOU].

[YOU+IMAGINE] [DIDN'T+UNDERSTAND?]
[HOW+ME+KNOW?] [EVIDENCE] [LITTLE]

[WANT+TO+SAY (stuck)]
[EVIDENCE+ON+HAND] (look at hand) [COURT+LOOK+AT]
[HAND+FADE+AWAY]

[LATIN] [" "]

[TRANSLATE] [MEANS] [BODY] [DESTROY+++]
[PUT+IT+BACK+ON] [WHOLE+BODY]

[POSSIBLE??] (point to the body)

[WALL] [HEAD+HIT].   [ME+BLANK].

(point to the back of head) [CRAWL+OVER+CONFUSED]

[WALL][SLITERING+DOWN+LAY+DOWN].
(point to the head)[SENSE] (nod).

At Christmas, I would sit at the top of the stairs and call 'can I come down now' and my dad would say in a voice that was warm 'not yet' and I would move down one stair and call again 'can I come down now' and my dad would say in a voice that was warm 'not yet' and I would move down one stair and call again 'can I come down now' and my dad would say in a voice that was warm 'not yet' and I would move down one step and one step until eventually I was at the very bottom and I could see the presents laid out on the table; one side for me and one side for my sister. We were a nice family.

Are you keeping up with this?

Is this what you prepared for?

What you expected to happen?

Is this beyond the realm of your experience?

Do you have the appropriate schema in place?

I'm talking to you now
Directly to you

Do you have the faintest idea of what I am talking about?
And how will I know?
When there is so very little evidence.

I am looking for the necessary narrative
Nothing I am saying would stand up in court

RESTITUTION IN INTEGRUM
There is a Latin phrase which translated means restoration to the whole.

Do you think that is too much to ask for?

My back hit the wall.
Then there is a blank.
But I make sense of the blank by making the memory
an organised whole
I see myself slithering down the wall to the floor.
That makes sense.
On some level that makes sense.

[ME+WATCH+TV] (describe) [COWBOY] [OPEN+DOORS]
[PULL+GUNS+OUT] [FIGHT+++] [HIT+OUT]
[SLITERING+DOWN] [GRAB(placement)+IN(head)].
C.R.U.M.P.L.E.D. (describe) [HEAD+DOWN]

[GOOD++]. [CAPTURE].   [THANK+YOU].
[ME+APPRECIATE+US+DISCUSS]

[APPRECIATE+YOU+HERE].
[APPRECIATE+YOU+HERE+LINK].

[THAT'S+IT+WAY]. [DIRECT]. [TELL+YOU+THANK+YOU].

[PROCESS] [NO+NEED].

I must have slithered, like a cowboy in a barroom brawl.
I crumpled.
Let's see what you do with crumpled

That's very good.
That captures it.
Thank you.
I really appreciate what you are doing
I really appreciate your being here.
I really appreciate your being here with me.
That's to you by the way. Directly to you. I am saying thank you.

It doesn't need interpreting.

SUE MACLAINE

NADIA speaks and SUE signs.

I just want you to come here.

Be here.

With me

I can see you are upset and that upsets me

I don't understand why you are crying.

Why are you crying?

Was it something I said?

Was it something I did?

You just have to know that you are a fucking little whore

Do you know that?

Do you?

Why are you such a slow learner?

Large bell.

[W++SAID]

[DUCK] [RABBIT] [DUCK (head move side down) RABBIT]

RABBIT (head move side down) DUCK]

[RABBIT (shake head) NOT+DUCK]
[DUCK (shake head) NOT+RABBIT]
(each handshape signs different) [RABBIT+DUCK]
[DUCK (smile)]
[RABBIT (sad)]
[NOT+DUCK]
[NOT+RABBIT]
[NOT+LAMP]

(describe Rolf Harris) [TELL+ME+WHATS+IT?]
[TELL+ME+WHATS+IT?] [CAN+YOU?]
[CAN+I?] [CAN+I+ANNOUNCE?] [CAN+I?]
[CAN+I?] [CAN+I+ANNOUNCE?] [CAN+I?]

(placement) [DUCK] [RABBIT]. (point at for which one)
[MIND+CONFUSED].
[DECIDE+THIS+ONE]
(placement) [DUCK] [RABBIT]. (point at for which one)

[MIND+CONFUSED].
[DECIDE+THIS+ONE]
[BECOME+EASY]
(tap on chest) [ME+DUCK] (tap on chest) [ME+RABBIT]
[ALL+FROM+PAST] [STOP]

Wittgenstein said

'INSTEAD OF ASKING WHAT IS THE MEANING OF A WORD,
WE SHOULD BE ASKING WHAT IS IT TO EXPLAIN
THE MEANING OF THE WORD'

Duck/Rabbit picture
[S] duckrabbit duckrabbit duckrabbit duckrabbit duckrabbit

It is a duck
It is a rabbit
It is a duck but it could also be a rabbit
It is a rabbit but it could also be a duck
It is a rabbit and not a duck
It is a duck and not a rabbit
It is both a rabbit and a duck

It is a happy duck
It is an unhappy rabbit
It is not a duck
It is not a rabbit
It is not a lamp

Can you tell what it is yet?   Can you tell what it is?   Can you tell?
Can we tell what it is yet?   Can we tell what it is?   Can we tell?
Can I tell what it is yet?   Can I tell what it is?   Can I tell?

A duck or a rabbit. It is one or the other
The mind cannot allow for nothing.
It has to be something
A duck or a rabbit.
It is one or the other
The mind cannot allow for nothing.
It has to be something
And so to make things easier:
(shouts) I am the duck and I am the rabbit
And now all of this can stop

[EVERYONE+KNOW+IMAGINE]
[KNOW+WHAT'S+GOING+ON]
[W+SAID]

[BED][TABLE] [ME+LOOK] [LAMP(describe)]
[LAMP(describe)] [WHY] [CAN'T+SAY+DAD]
(point)[DAD] D.A.D

(receptive)
[ME+PAUSE] [GOT+IT]
[STARE++]
[STARE++]
(hands down and stare)
(confused)
[LAMP] [HATE] (signs in slow motion and flick)
[LAMP+HOLD] [TWIST] [CRUMP+INTO+PIECES]
[CLEAN+UP] (look at the side)

STARE]
[STARE+++] [FINALLY] [LAMP+FADE+AWAY]

[HE+TOLD+ME+SH+++] (signs down)
[ME+DAUGHTER?]   [(shake head)ME+DAUGHTER+NO]
[D+FADE+AWAY]

[YOU+LOOK+AWAY][WHY?]
[YOU+SHUT+AWAY][WHY?]
[LANGUAGE] [SIGNS++] [FROZEN(stuck)] [HIT+WALL?]
[TIME] [SILENCE] [SPREAD+OUT?]
[HOW+LONG?]
[ONE+MINUTE?] (head down)
[OR] [TWO+MINUTES?] (head down)

Everyone knows where they are
Knows their place.
Wittgenstein said

> WHAT IS INCOMPREHENSIBLE IS THAT NOTHING
> AND YET EVERYTHING HAS CHANGED.
> THAT IS THE ONLY WAY TO PUT IT.

I looked at the lamp on the bedside table and I said lamp
I said lamp because I could not say dad
That's dad   D.a.d

I'll just pause while that is interpreted (3)
And I said it again
And I said it again
Until the lamp became independent from what it signified,
I negated the lamp.
I leapt over reality.   I flew.

I disintegrated it all. I annihilated the lamp.
Deprived it of its very being
I said lamp and I continued until finally the lamp was no longer
a lamp
He said quiet.
He said quiet and continued until finally I was no longer a daughter

Why have you stopped translating?
Why have you stopped translating?
Have we reached the limits of language?
Is it time to let silence speak?
For how long?
One minute? Or two?

(describe) [BUGLES] [TRUMPET]
[FLAG+DOWN] [FOLD] [PEOPLE-LINE] [GUNS+FIRED]
[CANNONS-LINE]
[MAYBE+FLOWERS]
[FLOWERS+WRAP] [FLOWERS+PULL+OFF]
[DROP+OFF+SPREAD+OUT] (signs over the space)
[DAISIES] [LILIES] [ROSES] [RED+POPPIES]
[RED+POPPY(location-heart)] [SURVIVOR]
[RED+POPPIES+WATERFALL+DOWN+IN-LINES+++]

[STATUE]
[PYRAMID]
[TEMPLE]

[NAMES ON LIST++++++]
[LIST+DOWN+++++]
[PHOTO][GALLERY+++]
[TREE][HANGING++]

[ROAD] [FLOWERS+PUT+DOWN]
[PATCH+SEW+TOGETHER+++]
[MEMORIAL+WALL]

[SOLIDERS+PARADE+MARCH+++]
[RELIGIOUS+LECTURE+++]
[SING++]

[SET+UP][CHOIR+SING++]
[THIS+CHRISTMAS+NUMBER+1]

[WATCH+TV][SPECIAL+MEMORIES]
[APOLOGY?]
[WILL+SAME?+++] [NOD++++]

[BELL] [PULL(x3)] [BELL+RINGS+++]

Will there be bugles and trumpets
Flags folded and guns fired
Will there be cannons
Will there be flowers
Bunches bought or clumped from the wild
Spilling over curbs
Daisies, lilies, roses, poppies
One for each survivor
Will there be a cascade
A waterfall?
Will there be a statue
A pyramid
A temple

Will names be written
Infinite in number?
Photographs in a gallery
or pinned flapping to a tree?

Will a roadside offering be made?
A patchwork quilt?
A memorial wall?

Will there be a parade for our wounded
A litany
A hymn

Will we form a choir?
Have a Christmas No 1

Will a special service be televised across the world?
Will there be an apology
Will there be a reckoning
Will there be a place of reckoning?
Will there be bells?

[THANK+YOU]
[NOW+GO+TO+END]
[BETTER+STOP]
[PLEASURE+YOU+HERE+LINK+ME]
[THIS(point at script)++]
[FIRST+TIME+TELL+YOU][NEVER+DONE+BEFORE].

[ME+LIKE+TELL+YOU+LAST+QUOTE+FROM+W+]

Thank you
We are coming to the end of our time together
We will have to stop
It has been an absolute pleasure to be here with you
To talk in this way
It doesn't happen very often.

I will finish with a quote from Wittgenstein
w.i.t.t.g.e.n.s.t.e.i.n

Choreographic sequence.

WWW.OBERONBOOKS.COM

Follow us on www.twitter.com/@oberonbooks
& www.facebook.com/OberonBooksLondon